More Welcome Speeches
and Responses
for All Occasions

More Welcome
Speeches
and Responses
for All Occasions

MORE WELCOME SPEECHES AND RESPONSES
FOR ALL OCCASIONS

Copyright © 1997 by Abingdon Press

ISBN 0-687-05298-X

ACKNOWLEDGMENTS

Welcome addresses on pages 9-23 are by Carol Overton. Used by permission.
Welcome Speeches by Children on pages 49-52 are by Dixie Phillips. Used
by permission.
Scripture quotations are from the King James or Authorized version of
the Bible.

03 04 05 06—10 9 8 7

MANUFACTURED IN THE UNITED STATES OF AMERICA

CONTENTS

SOME GENERAL WORDS
OF WELCOME

It is always a wonderful day when friends and loved ones can come together to worship and fellowship with God in peace and harmony. Today, we here at _____ would like to say welcome to each one of you visiting with us in the house of the Lord. Welcome.

First of all, giving honor to God, the giver of life, the pilot of our journey, we are truly honored to have each of you here today to celebrate this _____ anniversary of our church. We are especially honored to have with us (*here mention any visiting dignitaries from state or local offices, pastors from other churches, other special visitors*). It is indeed a pleasure for you to share this day with our church family. Words alone are not enough to welcome you, so at this time, please stand, turn to the person beside you, give that person a big hug and say, "You are welcome!"

This is the most wonderful day of our lives when friends and loved ones can come together to worship and fellowship with God in peace and harmony. Today, we here at _____ church would like to say welcome to each one of you visiting with us in the Lord's house. Welcome.

We are here today because of God's goodness. We are here because God rejoined us together in faith and love, to lift up bowed heads, to bring joy to those who are sad.

Today is a very special day in our church. It is people like you, our guests, who make this day special. Our faith unites us. Let us come together and praise the Lord with a new spirit. You are welcome here today.

God welcomes us into the kingdom. I am here today to welcome you into God's house of worship. Praise his name above all and give him honor.

We hope you find today to be an enjoyable experience. Feel free to clap your hands and lift them high in praise of God's holy name. We rejoice in all of God's goodness. Welcome.

Our goal today is to make a joyful noise unto the Lord. Anytime our doors are open, you are welcome to join in praising our savior. Because of God's goodness, love, and mercy, we can all praise God together in one mind and body.

That is why we say, "Welcome to our church, praise God!

You are welcome here not once, but twice."

It is indeed an honor and a pleasure to come to you on this very special occasion. We are gathered here today in God's most holy place to bring you a big welcome from our church family to yours. From our pastor I bring you these words of welcome, "For God so loved the world, that he gave his only begotten son," and again brothers and sisters in Christ, you are welcome.

First of all, giving honor to God and our pastor and other pulpit guests, we here at _____ bid each of you welcome. For God so loved the world, he gave his only begotten son, that we might fellowship in peace and harmony with one another. Our welcome comes from our heart and our hearts belong to God, and all of God's children are welcome.

Jesus said: "I am the bread of Life; those who come to me shall not hunger, and those who believe in me shall never thirst." I bid you welcome here today and pray that our time together will be as a well, full of the good news from Jesus and that when you leave you will be neither hungry nor thirsty.

Welcome!

The people you see around you are people who chose to come into the house of the Lord. There is no real need to say, "Welcome," because we know that we are always welcome in God's house of worship. No matter who we are, no matter what color we are, no matter how we came to believe in our savior, God will welcome us just as we are.

Still we want to add our words of welcome today. We are happy you are here. Welcome.

Welcome!

We are happy to join in fellowship with each of you today. We hope today will be a time of enjoyment and refreshing ourselves in the Lord. We hope that each person present will feel the overflow of love from our hearts.

We are happy to greet you with our love and joy and to remember that the Lord will greet each of us one day in that same way. You are welcome.

Today is a very special day at our church just because you are here. We are always welcome in the Lord's house and that welcome comes not only from church members, but from the Lord himself. We are surrounded by joy and love.

Whatever is ours around here we've offered for your use. Our task today is to make you feel at home in God's house. Please let us know if there is anything we can do to make this place of worship more welcoming to you. We do welcome you in the name of our Lord and Savior, Jesus Christ. Welcome.

God has set his glory above the heavens. When I consider the heavens, the work of God's hands, I am amazed. God created this great land in all its beauty. We come together today to praise God's holy name. We raise our hands in praise, knowing we are welcome in the land that God made and in God's house. Welcome.

Today is special.
It is the day that the Lord has made.
Let us rejoice and be glad in it.
Today is a most special day because of our guests.
We all can come together in the house of the Lord
    and feel his welcoming presence.
Welcome, our friends and visitors.

Leo Tolstoy once said, "All people live, not by reason of any care they have for themselves, but by the love for them that is in other people." Our Lord spoke to his followers, time after time, about the importance of loving others and of caring for others. We are a loving, caring, church. Your presence with us today is very important to us. We welcome you here in the name of Jesus Christ our Lord, and promise you that we will make every effort to care for you just as he asked us to. Welcome.

An old proverb says, "Make new friends, but keep the old; one is silver, the other gold." I see many old friends in the congregation today, and I see many people I am anxious to welcome as new friends. We do not say, "Welcome" lightly, but we speak that word from hearts of sincerity. We welcome you into God's house. Welcome, new friends and old!

Wait on the Lord everybody!
His love is so wonderful!
Come join us in praise!
Our doors are open to all;
Each of you is welcome in God's house.

A GENERAL RESPONSE

Thank you, (Sister/Brother) _____, for those words of welcome. This is indeed the day the Lord has made! We are delighted to be here to rejoice with you. I am _____ and have been chosen to respond to the welcome. On behalf of my pastor, other pastors (*names, if known*), and all guests present, I accept your heartfelt welcome. Thank you.

WELCOME SPEECHES
AND RESPONSES
FOR SPECIFIC OCCASIONS

CHILDREN'S DAY

Welcome to our church today. Today is a very special day. We are celebrating Children's Day, for we know God loves the little children, and we love having each of you here today. Having you here with us means so much, you are a part of us joined by God in love and faith. Welcome.

YOUTH SUNDAY

Today is Youth Sunday and I am delighted to extend the hand of friendship to every young person visiting here today. God is a welcome mat of all people. Don't worry about your religious experience, it makes no difference in your welcome here today. Your being here has made a difference in our church service. Welcome each of you.

MOTHER'S DAY

Welcome to this special day of celebration, Mother's Day. As I look out over those assembled here today, I see many families gathered to honor their mothers. I see others wearing flowers that signify that their mothers are now living in the land beyond the river. And I see "Other Mothers." "Other Mothers" are those special women who invest their love and life into children through their work in the church, as schoolteachers, or as special friends to neighborhood children. They may be biological mothers, or they may not, but these "Other Mothers" are extremely important to us. On behalf of each family represented here today, I welcome you to this celebration.

RESPONSE

As I think about all the women assembled here today, I am reminded of Eunice in the New Testament. We read about her in 2 Timothy. Eunice was not a great missionary, she did not start churches, she was neither an author nor an outstanding business-woman. But she is exalted in the New Testament because, like our mothers and "Other Mothers," she passed on her faith to her child. In honor of Eunice and of all the women gathered here, I accept your words of welcome.

FATHER'S DAY

Welcome

I am honored to have been asked to offer to you words of welcome on this special day, Father's Day. We especially welcome _____ (*list any visiting pastors or churches*), and all fathers present. Throughout the Old and New Testaments we are reminded to honor our parents and as we do so today, we also thank God for all those men who, though not our biological fathers, have cared for us. We know that the Lord is at work in building this "house" because of the dedicated men who daily labor to bring about the Kingdom of God on earth. In the names of those men, and in the name of God, the parent of us all, I welcome you to this day of worship.

RESPONSE

Thank you, (Sister/Brother) _____, for those inspiring words. We are glad to be here to honor those men who nurture this church. On behalf of all gathered here and in the name of God, the parent of us all, I accept your welcome.

GRADUATE RECOGNITION DAY

Welcome

Honored guests _____, and our graduates, I am delighted to have been chosen to extend our welcome to you. We have watched you grow from tiny babies to adults ready to take your place in our world. This church has been involved in your lives and we do not wish to end that involvement now. We will always be here, ready to encourage, to lend support, to uphold you with our prayers. The hope of our future is our children, and especially you, who we honor at this graduation celebration. Welcome.

Response

In First Corinthians we read, "When I was a child, I spake as a child, I understood as a child, I thought as a child: but when I became an [adult], I put away childish things. For now we see through a glass, darkly; but then face to face: now I know in part; but then shall I know even as also I am known" (1 Cor. 13:11-12). I am honored to be able to respond to the words of welcome from (Sister/Brother) _____. I do know in part what our young people will soon be facing and I know how important it will be to them to have the love and support of their church. No matter our age, we are still children of the heavenly king, and in the name of that king I say, "Thank you for having us here today."

DEACON ORDINATION

Welcome

Honored guests _____ (*list*), I am Deacon _____ and it is my pleasure to welcome you here today to celebrate the ordination of _____. As you know, deacons and pastors are called by God to be partners in ministry. No pastor alone can fulfill all the obligations and needs of the church; leadership, proclaiming the gospel, caring ministries. So into this partnership with God we also have deacons, ready to serve God and the church along side the pastor. Today we welcome you here for this celebration and we welcome _____ into the divine partnership. We are all servants of the Living Lord, and it is in His name that I welcome you here today.

Response

Thank you Deacon _____ for those inspiring words. I accept your welcome and on behalf of all those gathered here, I affirm our own partnership with the Living Lord. Thank you.

PASTOR ANNIVERSARY/ APPRECIATION

Welcome

Honored guests, pastor (*guest preacher*), choirs (*other special guests*), and especially our pastor's family, I am happy to welcome you to this very special day in the life of our church. _____ years ago the Lord blessed our congregation by sending to us his undershepherd, Pastor _____.

In Romans the apostle says, How then shall they call on him in whom they have not believed? And how shall they believe in him of whom they have not heard? And who shall they hear without a preacher? (Romans 10:14)

We are indeed fortunate that the Lord saw fit to send Pastor _____ to preach the good news. Pastor _____ is the Lord's representative here on earth.

The task of a preacher is not an easy one, and the responsibilities are large. For this reason, we also want to say a special word of appreciation to our pastor's family. Thank you.

Again, I say "welcome" to you who have joined us today. May you leave here filled with the fruit of the spirit.

Response

(Sister/Brother) _____, what beautiful words of welcome. Thank you. I am _____ and have been chosen to respond to the welcome. We are honored to be here today to celebrate with you your years with one who so ably represents Christ in the affairs of the Kingdom on earth.

CHOIR DAY

Welcome

"Make a joyful noise unto God, all ye lands: Sing forth the honor of his name: make his praise glorious" (Psalm 66:1-2). Welcome honored guests (*here list the guest preacher and choir, musicians, soloists, and visitors who are present. If charter members of any of choirs are present, they should be recognized*), it is my privilege to welcome you to this day of praise. Today marks the _____ year that the _____ choir has been making a joyful noise in honor of God's name. I bid you welcome in their name and in the hope that today will be a special blessing to you. Welcome.

Response

Thank you for those words of welcome. Until we are gathered with the saints in glory, singing that wondrous story, we take great pleasure in singing the Lord's praises here on earth. It is indeed a privilege to join with all assembled here today to mark this anniversary and to lift our voices with yours.

MISSIONS

Jesus said, "Ye are the light of the world. A city that is set on a hill cannot be hid. Neither do men light a candle, and put it under a bushel, but on a candlestick; and it giveth light unto all that are in the house. Let your light so shine before men, that they may see your good works, and glorify your Father which is in heaven (Matthew 5:14-16).

We come together today to join in a common project. We want not only to relieve some of the suffering in our land and in the world, but through our actions to draw others to the lamb of God. It is my pleasure to welcome you here today. I see reflected in your faces, the light of the world. May we go forth from this place, and give light to all the world.

FOR CHRISTIAN UNITY

Welcome to this house of the Lord. We meet here today to celebrate God's love, poured out on all peoples. When God set the rainbow in the sky, it was a sign of the covenant God has established between God and *all life on earth.* We come today to re-affirm that covenant. It is in the name of Jesus, who unites us all, that I welcome you here today.

The Bible says, "The Spirit himself testifies with our spirit that we are God's children" (Romans 8:16). It is as a child of God and as your sibling that I welcome you to God's house today. If there is anything we can do to make this a more enjoyable experience for you, please ask. Welcome.

45

WELCOME SPEECHES
GIVEN BY CHILDREN

SO GLAD

I'm so glad we can be together on this special holiday!

Pastor _____ is so glad you've come to hear what we have to say!

One thing is for certain, I have not one single doubt,

Our _____ (*type of play*) will make you want to clap and shout!

A SECRET

I have a secret I want to share,
I know how Pastor _____ got from here (*point to pew*) to there (*point to pulpit*).

It all started up here in front of people like you.
Back then, he was just a little fella, barely more than two.
He stood up real tall and said his part;
That's when the Lord spoke to his heart.
I wonder what the Lord has for me?
I guess we'll all just have to wait and see!
So remember as you're watching our _____ (*type of play*) play,
All our little lives are being molded like clay.
And when we cause you grief and frustration,
Remember (*point up*) we're carrying God's light to our generation!

TOO LITTLE

I'm too little to drive a car,
That's what Mama and Daddy say.
But I'm not too little to
Welcome you to our _____(*type of play*) Play!

ABOUT TO START

Children dressed in angel wings,
Recite lines and someone sings,
Mamas smile and Daddies grin,
As our Christmas play begins.
Sit back and let us warm your heart,
Our Christmas play's about to start!

(Hold up "Welcome" sign)

POETRY
AND
PRAYERS

Holy, holy, holy is the Lord God Almighty,
who is, who was and who is to come.
Let us praise and glorify him for ever.
You are worthy, Lord our God,
to receive praise and glory,
honor and blessing.
Let us praise and glorify him for ever.
Worthy is the Lamb that was slain to receive
divine power, wisdom and strength,
honor, glory and blessing.
Let us praise and glorify him for ever.
Bless the Lord
all your works of the Lord. Let us praise and glorify
him for ever.
Praise our God all you his servants,
honor him, you who fear God, small and great.
Let us praise and glorify him for ever.
Let heaven and earth praise your glory:
all creatures in heaven, on earth and under the earth,
the sea and everything in it.
Let us praise and glorify him for ever.

St. Francis of Assisi
1182–1226

Jesus asks, "What do you have that will last forever?" Will your home, your clothing, your treasures of silver and gold? Will your car, your fine linen and silk?"

"No," we hear the answer echoing down the ages. "You can be sure of only one thing, the love I had for you when I died for you on Calvary's cross."

Almighty and most merciful God, who has given us a new commandment that we should love one another, give us all grace to fulfill it. Make us gentle, courteous, and forebearing. Direct our lives so that we may look to the good of others in word and deed. Hallow all our friendships by the blessing of thy Spirit, for the sake of your Son Jesus Christ our Lord.

Bishop Westcott
1825–1901

JESUS WILL SUSTAIN YOU

Does the world no rest afford?
Would you have your strength restored?
Cast your burden on the Lord,
Jesus will sustain you.

Are you tempted by the foe?
Has your burden laid you low?
To the one true Helper go,
Jesus will sustain you.

Are you weary of the fray?
Have you fallen by the way?
Make the Savior yours today,
Jesus will sustain you.

Jesus will sustain you,
Jesus will sustain you;
When you need a Friend to help you,
Jesus will sustain you.

James Rowe

THE HOUR OF PRAYER

Glory to God for the joy to meet,
Here at the hour of prayer;
Welcome the bliss of communion sweet,
Here at the hour of prayer.

Far from the world we may turn away,
Here at the hour of prayer;
Gladly we rest from the toils of the day,
Here at the hour of prayer.

Rich are the blessings that all may seek,
Here at the hour of prayer;
Grace for the weary, the faint, the weak,
Here at the hour of prayer.

O what a holy and calm repose,
Here at the hour of prayer;
Love in its fullness the heart o'er flows,
Here at the hour of prayer.

Nearer the gate to the soul's bright home,
Near the vales where the faithful roam,
Nearer to God and the Lamb we come,
Here at the hour of prayer.

Fanny J. Crosby

REMEMBERED

Fading away, like the stars of the morning,
Losing their light in the glorious sun;
So let me steal away, gently and lovingly,
Only remembered by what I have done.

So in the harvest, if others may gather
Sheaves from the fields that in spring I have sown;
Who plowed or sowed matters not to the reaper:
I'm only remembered by what I have done.

Fading away, like the stars of the morning,
So let my name be unhonored, unknown;
Here, or up yonder, I must be remembered,
Only remembered by what I have done.

EASTER

The city streets of Easter, they heard his step, I know,
Through dusky, purpled pavements, past twinkling
    lights aglow,
For every gleaming blossom shop that opened to the
    night,
Was sweet with Easter fragrance and lilies tall and
    white.
The furred and broad-clothed people beneath the
    arc-lit skies,
Bore something new and tender and giving in their eyes;
Down every dingy alleyway rang children's laughter
    glad
And weary, work-worn faces smiled less wistfully
    and sad;
Each sooty, cinder-laden breeze seemed cleansed by
    robes of snow;
The city streets of Easter—they heard his step, I know.

The country roads of Easter, they felt his footsteps
    pass;
They watched through greening meadows
    the windless, stirring grass;
The buds broke into leaf mist along the poplared hill;
the bluebirds rippled homing note, the red-winged
    black- bird's thrill,
The first lone thrush note, silver soft through
    hemlock boughs astart,

Held sudden joy so piercing sweet it brushed the
naked heart;
And down the roadway's southern banks from
brown, earth-scented sod,
There blossomed frail white bloodroot star,
Like fingerprints of God;
Each tiny hill-farm window shone with sunset-
gloried glass;
The country roads of Easter, they felt his footsteps pass.

But oh, the pathways of my heart, they knew Him
most of all!
They saw no jeweled city lights, they heard no
bluebird's call.
But sudden-sweet as lily breath through winter dusk
I knew
That Death was but the gathered dreams of Life and
Love come true;
That never faith went unfulfilled, that never hope
was vain,
That never hands are parted but will grip with hand
again—
One passed in the dawning, and all the road He went
Was bright with Easter sunshine, and sweet with lily
scent;
Oh, roads of dew-fresh morning, or city evenfall,
My heart's small hidden pathways,
They knew Him most of all.

Martha Haskell Clark

Who hath not learned, in hours of faith,
The truth to flesh and sense unknown,
That Life is ever lord of Death,
And Love can never lose its own!

John Greenleaf Whittier